Be An Expert!™

Farm Animals

Amy Edgar

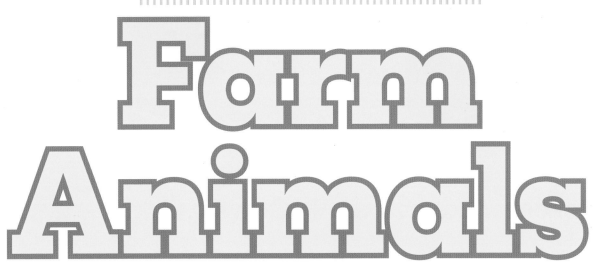

Children's Press®
An imprint of Scholastic Inc.

Contents

Know the Names

Be an expert! Get to know the names of these farm animals.

Chickens

Chickens scratch and peck.
Some lay eggs.

Barn Buzz

Q: How many eggs can a chicken lay?

A: Most female chickens, called hens, can lay an egg almost every day.

Cows

Cows are **herbivores.**
They eat mostly grass.

Moooo!

Expert Fact

A dairy cow can produce more than seven gallons of milk a day. That is more than 100 glasses!

Goats

They like to live in big groups.
Baby goats are called kids.

Maaaaa!

Zoom In

Find these parts in the big picture.

beard   **hooves**   **eyes**   **horns**

Pigs

They use their **snouts** to smell and to dig.

Barn Buzz

Q: Why do pigs wallow, or roll in the mud?

A: It helps them keep cool.

Oink, oink!

Sheep

Their bodies are covered in soft wool.

Baaaa!

Sheep are not hurt when their wool is **sheared**, or cut off. It's like getting a haircut. Wool is made into yarn to make warm sweaters.

Dogs

Dogs **herd** and protect other farm animals.

Woof, woof!

Barn Buzz

Q: How do dogs herd sheep?

A: Some dogs bark, nip, and run to help move the sheep. They might herd them toward more food or back to the farm.

Horses

They are strong and fast.

Neigh!

Zoom In

Find these parts in the picture.

mane   **tail**   **muzzle**

Rabbits

They have strong back legs.
They use them to hop.

All the Farm Animals

They do many things on the farm. Thanks, farm animals!

1.

2.

5.

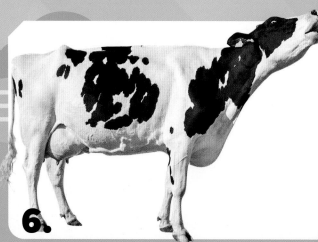

6.

Expert Quiz

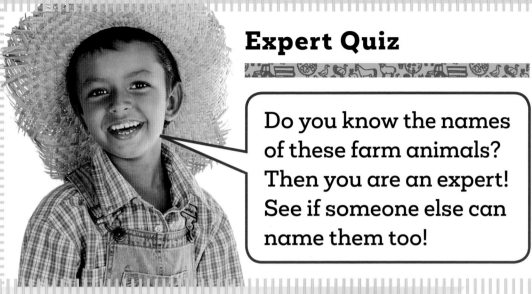

Do you know the names of these farm animals? Then you are an expert! See if someone else can name them too!

3.

4.

7.

8.

Answers: 1. Rabbit. 2. Chicken. 3. Dog. 4. Horse. 5. Sheep. 6. Cow. 7. Pig. 8. Goat.

21

Expert Gear

Meet a farmer. What does she need to take care of animals on the farm?

She has a **hat**.

She has **tools**.

She has a **barn**.

She has a **tractor**.

Glossary

herbivores (HUR-buh-vorz): animals that eat only plants.

herd (HURD): to move animals together in a group. The dog herds the sheep.

sheared (SHEERD): cut the hair or wool off a sheep or other animal.

snouts (SNOUTS): the parts of animals' faces that include the nose and mouth.

Index

Library of Congress Cataloging-in-Publication Data
Names: Edgar, Amy, author.
Title: Farm animals / Amy Edgar.
Description: New York: Children's Press, an imprint of Scholastic Inc., 2021. | Series: Be an expert! | Includes index. | Audience: Ages 4-5. |
Audience: Grades K-1. | Summary: "Book introduces the reader to farm animals"— Provided by publisher.
Identifiers: LCCN 2020031790 | ISBN 9780531136713 (library binding) | ISBN 9780531136720 (paperback)
Subjects: LCSH: Domestic animals—Juvenile literature. | Livestock—Juvenile literature.
Classification: LCC SF75.5 .E34 2021 | DDC 63—dc23
LC record available at https://lccn.loc.gov/2020031790

Printed in Heshan, China 62

SCHOLASTIC, CHILDREN'S PRESS, BE AN EXPERT!™, and associated logos are trademarks and/or registered trademarks of Scholastic Inc.

1 2 3 4 5 6 7 8 9 10 R 30 29 28 27 26 25 24 23 22 21

Scholastic Inc., 557 Broadway, New York, NY 10012.

Art direction and design by THREE DOGS DESIGN LLC.

Photos ©: cover sky: Evgeniya Tiplyashina/123rf; cover cow: Alan Hopps/Getty Images; cover grass: almoond/Getty Images; 1 cow: Claudius Thiriet/Biosphoto; 2 top right: Isselee/Dreamstime; 3 center left: Agency Animal Picture/Getty Images; 5 sidebar top: FatCamera/Getty Images; 7 sidebar right: Westend61/Getty Images; 7 bottom right: Jean-François Noblet/Biosphoto; 8 bottom: Yann Avril/Biosphoto; 9 sidebar top: April Burns/Offset; 9 sidebar center left, sidebar right: Yann Avril/Biosphoto; 11 sidebar top: kali9/Getty Images; 11 sidebar bottom: fatihhoca/Getty Images; 15 sidebar top: RichVintage/Getty Images; 17 sidebar top: Glenda Powers/Dreamstime; 18 bottom: Natthapon M/Dreamstime; 18-19: Agencja Fotograficzna Caro/Alamy Images; 19 sidebar: AzmanL/Getty Images; 20 top left: Natthapon M/Dreamstime; 20 bottom right: Claudius Thiriet/Biosphoto; 21 center left: Agency Animal Picture/Getty Images.

All other photos © Shutterstock.